I0755005

WNBA
CONNECTICUT SUN
Mitchell Lane
PUBLISHERS
Nancy Coffelt

Mitchell Lane
PUBLISHERS

mitchelllanepub.com

2001 SW 31st Avenue
Hallandale, FL 33009

First Edition, 2026.
Author: Nancy Coffelt
Designer: Ed Morgan
Editor: Tammy Gagne

Series: WNBA
Title: Connecticut Sun

Library bound ISBN: 979-8-89260-475-8
eBook ISBN: 979-8-89260-495-6

Photo credits: p. 7, 9, 23, 25 wikimedia; balance Alamy

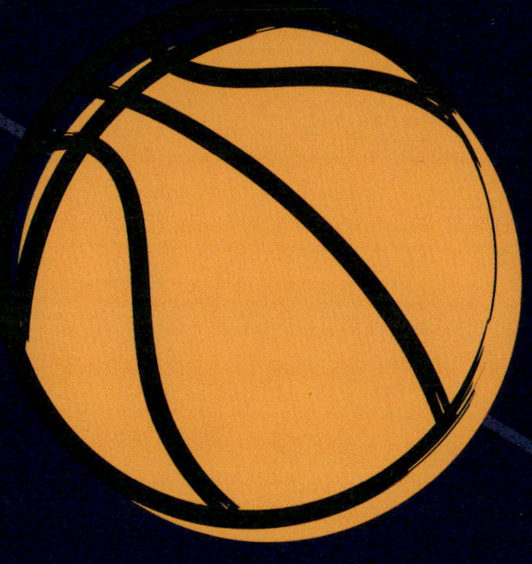

CONTENTS

Chapter ONE

HARD-FOUGHT WINS

DiJonai Carrington played college ball for Stanford and Baylor Universities.

The Connecticut Sun was off to a strong start for the 2024 season. The team had played five games and won all of them, including one in overtime. Sun players had fought hard for these wins. In every game they had come back from behind. "We have some of the toughest competitors that I've ever been around," Sun head coach Stephanie White told *CT Insider*. "But I don't feel like we've really played 40 minutes of our best basketball on both ends of the floor. We just haven't put it together."

CHAPTER ONE

On May 28, 2024, the Sun faced the Phoenix Mercury. The New England players were determined to hold onto their winning streak. They wanted to play their best 40 minutes of basketball. **Forward** Brionna Jones was returning after an **Achilles tendon** injury and surgery. But she was still limited on the total number of minutes she was allowed to play in each game. Jones came out strong, sinking 10 points in the first 13 minutes. She ended up scoring 15 points in her 18 minutes of play.

Hard-Fought Wins

FAST FACT

DeWanna Bonner set a new team record on June 8, 2023, when she scored 41 points in a single game.

CHAPTER ONE

Forward DeWanna Bonner led the scoring with 19 points. She had now surpassed 7,000 total career points, as just the fifth WNBA player to achieve this milestone. **Guard** DiJonai Carrington provided strong defense with a career-high 9 **rebounds**. At times, the Sun led the Mercury by as much as 26 points. The final score was 70–47. "I've been here a long time, so to start this way," Sun forward Alyssa Thomas told *CT Insider*, "[I]t speaks volumes to the kind of players we have here."

Hard-Fought Wins

DiJonai Carrington

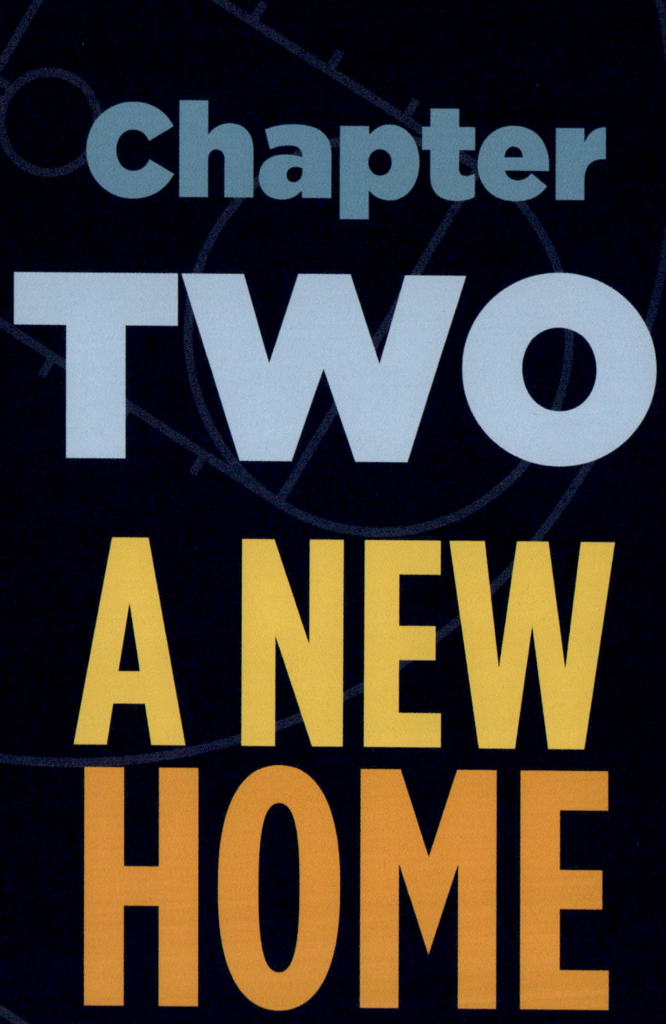

Chapter TWO

A NEW HOME

The Connecticut Sun mascot, Blaze, performs during a game.

The WNBA was created in 1996 with eight teams. In 1998, the league added two more, the Minnesota Lynx and the Orlando Miracle. But the Miracle wouldn't remain in Orlando, Florida. In 2003, the team was sold to the Mohegan Tribe in southeastern Connecticut, where it was renamed the Connecticut Sun.

CHAPTER TWO

The Sun was the first independently owned team in the WNBA. It was also the first professional sports team owned by an Indigenous tribe. The Mohegan Tribe also owns a popular casino called the Mohegan Sun. The Connecticut Sun plays at the casino's 10,000-seat arena in Uncasville. On the front of each player's uniform is the word *Keesusk*, which means "sun" in the Mohegan language.

The Sun has had ups and downs since its first season. There are two **conferences** in the WNBA. Six teams play for the Eastern Conference and six teams play for the Western Conference. The Sun has come in first for the Eastern Conference rankings five times, reaching the finals in both 2004 and 2005. The team has also come in last three times, between 2013 and 2015.

A New Home

Nykesha Sales is one of only three players in the League to have competed in every WNBA All-Star Game.

FAST FACT

With a win on August 9, 2006, the Sun celebrated 12 victories in a row. It was the third-longest winning streak in WNBA history at the time.

CHAPTER TWO

At the end of May 2024, the Sun's record was looking strong at 6–0. But Alyssa Thomas knew that she and the rest of the team needed to keep working hard instead of celebrating too soon. She told *CT Insider*. "We know it's a long season. So, it's not time for us to get comfortable or feed into that but just continue to do what we're doing."

It wasn't until 2019 that they were in the finals again. They made it there a fourth time in 2022. Heading into the 2024 playoffs, Coach Stephanie White was feeling positive about the Sun's defense. "It always takes a little bit of luck, right?" She told *The Next* website. "You [have got to] stay healthy. You [have got to] hit your stride. It's about **momentum** at the right time."

A New Home

Coach Stephanie White played for five seasons in the WNBA.

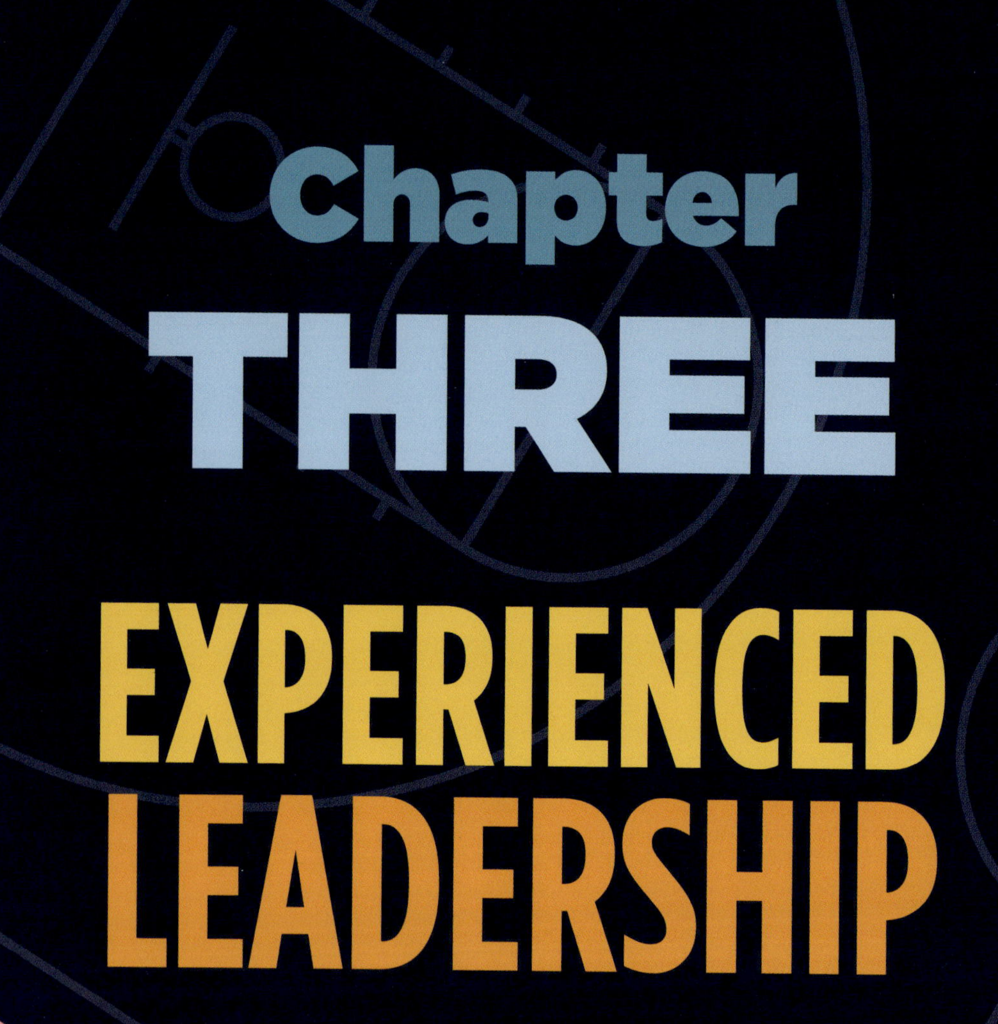

Chapter THREE

EXPERIENCED LEADERSHIP

In November 2024, Stephanie White was named head coach of the Indiana Fever.

Stephanie White became the Connecticut Sun's coach in November 2022. She brought extensive basketball experience to the job. White had spent four years playing college ball for Purdue University. In her senior year, she helped the team win the 1999 NCAA Championship and was named Big Ten Conference Player of the Year. In 1999, White began her WNBA career when she was drafted by the Charlotte Sting. After one season with the North Carolina team, she went on to play four more with the Indiana Fever. In 2006, White was **inducted** into the Purdue Athletics Hall of Fame.

CHAPTER THREE

White retired from playing in the WNBA in 2004 to coach college basketball. She then became an assistant coach for the Chicago Sky in 2007, staying in this role for the next three years. From 2011 to 2014, White worked as an assistant coach for the Fever. She rose to head coach in 2015, remaining in that position for two years. But college ball called her back in 2016. She was Vanderbilt University's head coach for the women's basketball team until 2021.

White's first season as the head coach for the Sun was a winning one. The team finished the regular season with 27 wins and 13 losses, setting a record for the Sun **franchise**. It took Connecticut to the playoffs, but the Sun lost to the Las Vegas Aces.

Experienced Leadership

With 379 regular season victories, Mike Thibault is the winningest coach in WNBA history.

FAST FACT

The Connecticut Sun's first head coach was Mike Thibault, who led the team to its early finals appearances.

CHAPTER THREE

Rachid Meziane took over as the head coach of the Sun ahead of the 2025 season. General manager Morgan Tuck was excited to welcome the new coach who came all the way from Europe. Meziane coached top women's teams in both France and Belgium. "He brings a wealth of experience, passion, and a proven track record of success that will help elevate our players and team as a whole," Tuck said in a statement.

Experienced Leadership

Rachid Meziane led Belgium to its first FIBA (International Basketball Federation) European Women's Gold Medal Championship in 2023.

Chapter FOUR

HERE COMES THE SUN

Forward Alyssa Thomas is a five-time WNBA All-Star.

Forward Alyssa Thomas played for the Sun from 2014 to 2024. She holds the team's records for rebounds and **assists**. In 2024, Thomas was chosen to play for Team USA at the Paris Olympics. It wasn't her first experience playing overseas. In 2022, Thomas helped bring home a gold medal for the United States at the FIBA Basketball World Cup in Australia.

CHAPTER FOUR

"I am honored to be selected to the USA Basketball Women's National Team and I am excited to compete at my first Olympics this summer," Thomas said in an interview with the WNBA ahead of the games. "It's a dream come true to have the opportunity to wear the USA jersey and I am looking forward to playing alongside the best players in the world on the biggest stage." She and Team USA won a gold medal in Paris as well.

After playing for Baylor University, DiJonai Carrington was drafted by the Sun in 2021. Three years later, Carrington was enjoying the best season of her WNBA career. As a guard, she specializes in defense. "The number one priority is bringing it on the defensive end of the floor, and she's doing that," Sun Head Coach Stephanie White told *The Next* website in 2024. Although she moved to the Dallas Wings for the 2025 season, Carrington gave the Sun her very best during her four seasons with the team.

Here Comes the Sun

FAST FACT

Forward Alyssa Thomas was named the Associated Press Comeback Player of the Year on August 16, 2022.

CHAPTER FOUR

Carrington is the daughter of former NFL player Darren Carrington. She credits her own background in football for developing her defending skills. She began playing flag football when she was seven. A year later, she convinced her father to let her play tackle football. One of the things she learned to do as a **defensive back** was read the offensive players' eyes.

The Connecticut Sun had a strong season in 2024. One of the top teams in the WNBA, they were rated number one in ESPN's WNBA Power Rankings. Roneeka Hodges joined the Sun as a new assistant coach ahead of the 2025 season. She said on the team's official website, "I look forward to sharing my knowledge of the game and experiences as we continue to grow a winning culture."

Here Comes the Sun

Roneeka Hodges played 297 games for five teams in her eleven-season WNBA career.

GLOSSARY

Achilles tendon
The tendon that connects the calf muscle in the lower leg to the heel bone

assists
Passes made to teammates, which lead to scored points

conference
A grouping of sports teams based on geography

defensive back
A football player positioned on the defensive side of the field, also called a safety

forward
A basketball player who plays near the basket, often rebounding and scoring points

franchise
A team in a professional sports league

guard
A basketball player who brings the ball up the court and sets up offensive plays

inducted
Admitted into an organization

momentum
Strength gained from continuing action

rebounds
Caught basketballs after missed shots

SLAM DUNK WNBA TRIVIA

- The Connecticut Sun's team colors are blue, red, and gold.
- The 2010 WNBA Rookie of the Year was Sun forward Tina Charles. She also won the WNBA Most Valuable Player (MVP) award in 2012.
- Guard Katie Davis played 14 seasons for the Connecticut Sun before retiring from the WNBA in 2015.
- After beating the New York Liberty on September 15, 2021, the Sun won 13 straight games, breaking its earlier record set in 2006.
- Jonquel Jones won the WNBA MVP award in 2021.
- Despite four appearances in the WNBA Finals, the Sun has yet to win a championship.

FIND OUT MORE

IN PRINT

Anderson, Josh. *Connecticut Sun*. Lerner Publications, 2025.

Orr, Tamra B. *Indiana* Fever. Mitchell Lane Publishers, 2026.

O'Neal, Ciara. *The WNBA Finals*. North Star Editions, 2023.

ON THE INTERNET

Connecticut Sun.
https://sun.wnba.com.

"Connecticut Sun," ***ESPN*, n.d.**
www.espn.com/wnba/team/_/name/conn/connecticut-sun.

"Connecticut Sun," ***FOX Sports*, n.d.**
www.foxsports.com/wnba/connecticut-sun-team.

INDEX

About the Author

Writer **Nancy Coffelt** has never played professional basketball, but she did win a free-throw contest in junior high school. Nancy lives, writes, and paints in eastern Oregon. She appreciates athletes and anyone else who follow their dreams and work hard to achieve their goals.